THE
ROYAL
FAMILY
A Year in Focus
PHOTOGRAPHED BY TIM GRAHAM

The Sandringham Flower Show

This colourful local show is held every year in the park of Sandringham House, the Queen's country estate in Norfolk. In 1984 both the Queen and the Queen Mother attended the show which is a favourite engagement of theirs. It is an informal occasion with plenty of time to study the various exhibitions and to talk to the crowds of spectators, most of whom are local inhabitants from the surrounding villages and from the nearby town of King's Lynn.

Polo tops the list of Prince Charles's activities and he plays regularly during the season as often as his many commitments permit. When spending weekends at Windsor Castle the Queen occasionally attends the polo matches at nearby Smith's Lawn. She enjoys meeting the teams and presenting the trophies. (*Left*) At the Cartier International Polo Day the Queen presented Prince Charles, whose team lost, with a consolation prize and he then delighted the spectators by kissing his mother's hand in return.

(*Below*) On 4 August the Queen Mother celebrated her 84th birthday at Clarence House. She made her customary visit to the crowds outside the gates who were waiting to wish her a happy birthday. (*Right*) Princess Margaret's children, Viscount Linley and his younger sister, Lady Sarah Armstrong-Jones, accompanied their grandmother when she went out to meet the well-wishers who included, as usual, many small children carrying bunches of flowers to present to the Queen Mother.

Prince Charles in Papua New Guinea

In August Prince Charles paid a five-day visit to Papua New Guinea, a member of the Commonwealth, to open the new £25-million Parliament building in Port Moresby, the capital. The visit was full of exotic moments for Prince Charles, who even took part in some of the native ceremonies, accepting garlands and necklaces from natives, joining in traditional chants and watching dancing displays by warriors with painted faces.

(*Left*) Garlanded with exotic frangipani flowers, Prince Charles watches a display of native dancing at Popondetta. (*Below and facing page*) On the island of Manus, Prince Charles was installed as the islanders' supreme chief or 'Lapan'. Wearing a crown and necklaces of dogs' teeth and brandishing a carved spear, Prince Charles greeted his new subjects in pidgin English.

Prince Henry Charles Albert David, to be known as Prince Harry, was born on Saturday, 15 September in the Lindo Wing of St Mary's Hospital, Paddington. The Prince weighed 6 lb 14 oz and is now the third in line of succession to the throne. (*Above*) The Prince and Princess of Wales leaving the Lindo Wing with their day-old son for the short return journey to Kensington Palace. (*Left*) Earlier in the day Prince Charles had brought Prince William to the hospital to visit his mother and new baby brother. He is seen here leaving the hospital with his nanny.

AUTUMN 1984

The Queen Mother visits Venice

In October the Queen Mother paid her long-awaited first visit to Venice, one of the most magical cities in the world, surrounded by its lagoon and many islands. The Queen Mother had been invited by The Venice in Peril Fund, a British organization and one of many whose aim is to help preserve the city's rich historic treasures and buildings. The Queen Mother spent three days sightseeing, staying on board the Royal Yacht *Britannia* which berthed in St Mark's Basin, in front of the Palace of the Doges.

(*Below and right*) In the autumn the mists hang low over the lagoon and the dozens of narrow canals. For the Queen Mother it was a unique and memorable experience as she sped from place to place in a Venetian 'water-taxi', carrying out her busy programme.

(*Left*) Accompanied by the Flag Officer of the Royal Yacht, the Queen Mother was taken for a short gondola ride along one of the narrow canals. (*Above*) A packed sightseeing programme included a stroll in front of the pinkish building of the Palace of the Doges. In the background can be seen a marble column crowned with the winged lion of St Mark, the city's patron saint. Everywhere she went the Queen Mother was greeted by crowds of enthusiastic Venetians and by tourists who, like herself, had come to marvel at the wonders of this famous city.

(*Left*) The Queen in jovial mood is welcomed by the Lord Mayor of London, Dame Mary Donaldson as she arrives at the steps of St Paul's Cathedral to attend a Service of Thanksgiving to mark the centenary of the National Society for the Prevention of Cruelty to Children of which the Queen is joint patron.

(*Below*) Every year the Queen drives in State to Westminster for the State Opening of Parliament. Occurring whenever there is a new session of Parliament, this year in November, it is an occasion of great pageantry and historic meaning. The Queen drives from Buckingham Palace to Westminster in the Irish State Coach, drawn by four horses, with a Sovereign's Escort of the Household Cavalry.

(*Right*) Many of the Princess of Wales's official engagements are connected with charities and organizations actively involved in helping babies and children. On her second official engagement after the birth of Prince Henry, she visited the Family Centre of SENSE, the National Deaf-Blind and Rubella Association in Ealing, West London. The Centre offers support and advice to families of young children who are born deaf and blind as a result of maternal rubella and other causes.

(*Below*) The Prince and Princess of Wales accompanied the Queen in the Irish State Coach to the State Opening of Parliament. For this formal occasion, the Princess had a new hairstyle, wearing it swept up at the back and sides, around the Spencer tiara.

(*Left*) The Princess of Wales visiting Wellingborough in Northamptonshire. The Princess spent the day meeting Asian and Afro-Caribbean ladies' groups.

(*Below*) The Princess of Wales on her first official engagement after the birth of Prince Henry seven weeks earlier. Greeted by the Mayor of Newham in East London, the Princess was visiting one of Dr Barnardo's youth projects, the Neville Road Centre.

(*Overleaf*) The Princess of Wales launching the luxurious new P & O liner, *Royal Princess*, in Southampton. *Royal Princess* is the most expensive passenger ship ever to be built in the world.

(*Facing page*) The Queen and Prince Philip paid a visit to the Medway towns in Kent at the end of October. Here, the Queen is surrounded by enthusiastic crowds waving thousands of Union flags on the walkabout down Rochester's refurbished Victorian High Street, decked with bunting.

At the end of November Princess Michael of Kent invited Tim Graham to take a series of family photographs at her country home of Nether Lypiatt Manor in Gloucestershire. Here, the Princess and her children, Lord Frederick Windsor, aged six and Lady Gabriella Windsor, aged four, can relax and enjoy an outdoor country life with their many animals, including Sponge, the yellow labrador, Lady Gabriella's pony Dominic and the Princess's pedigree Burmese and Siamese cats. Although married to Prince Michael of Kent, a cousin to the Queen, the Princess likes to remind her children of her own, and hence their mid-European ancestry. For part of the session the family dressed in traditional Austrian costume.

WINTER 1984-5

Princess Anne in the United Arab Emirates

In early December Princess Anne and Captain Mark Phillips paid a visit to Dubai, Abu Dhabi and Sharjah, carrying out a variety of engagements. The main reason for the trip was an invitation to the couple to co-star in the Dubai Horse Show.

(*Left and below*) Princess Anne at the opening ceremony of the Horse Show, talking to Sheikh Hasher Maktoum.

(*Facing page*) During the visit to Sharjah Princess Anne and Captain Mark Phillips toured the local *souq* or Arab street market and came away laden with Christmas presents for the family at home.

Princess Anne is an active
Colonel-in-Chief of the 14th/
20th King's Hussars. In
February she spent three
days on manoeuvres with
the regiment at Hohne in
North Germany, driving a
Scorpion light tank and also
inspecting the insides of and
driving a Chieftain tank, the
biggest in the British army.

(*Left*) The Princess of Wales leaving Cirencester Police Station after a visit to the headquarters of the Gloucestershire Constabulary where she had seen special exhibitions mounted for the occasion.

(*Below*) Wearing a favourite plaid suit, the Princess of Wales visited Swindon in February to visit the Taurus Training Workshop for school leavers to train in engineering and carpentry skills. The apprentices then sell their own products.

(*Facing page*) The Princess of Wales leaving Goldsmiths' Hall at the beginning of March after a private reception attended also by the Queen and the Prince of Wales to meet beneficiaries of the Royal Jubilee Trust. The Queen's Silver Jubilee Trust and the King George V Jubilee Fund were combined to form this trust whose aim is to help young people help others.

THE BRITISH
EMPIRE
1558-1983

To mark Prince Edward's 21st birthday on 10 March, Tim Graham was invited to take a series of photographs of the Prince in and around Jesus College, Cambridge where he is studying history. The Prince is now in his final year and has involved himself actively in student life so far, taking part in amateur dramatics and playing rugby for his college. When Prince Edward leaves Cambridge he will undertake training to become an officer in the Marines, one of the toughest jobs in the British forces.

(*Left and facing page*) On a bitterly cold and snowy day in February the Princess of Wales paid a visit to the Sobell Centre at the Churchill Hospital in Oxford. Sporting a three-quarter length royal blue suit and hat with black accessories the Princess was a bright figure on such a freezing day.

(*Right*) Both on and off-duty the Royal Family travel around the country mainly by aeroplane and helicopter. Here in March, Prince Henry has just completed his first flight on his way to Balmoral for a weekend with his family.

(*Left*) The Princess of Wales at the première of the film *Amadeus* in aid of the Royal College of Music Centenary Appeal. Wearing a stunning dark blue velvet dress, she also wore her Arabian sapphire and diamond necklace and earrings, a much-prized wedding present.

(*Facing page and right*) The Royal Film Performance has been an annual occasion since 1946 and this year the film chosen for this glittering event was the long-awaited *A Passage to India*, directed by Britain's most famous director, Sir David Lean and produced by Lord Brabourne, son-in-law of the late Earl Mountbatten. There was a good turn-out by the Royal Family to support the occasion, including the Queen Mother and Princess Anne, looking extremely elegant in grey silk moiré.

The Queen and Prince Philip's State Visit to Portugal

In March, amid the warm spring sunshine, the Queen and Prince Philip paid their second State Visit to Portugal, the first having taken place as long ago as 1957. Britain and Portugal have had close commercial ties for over six hundred years and Portugal was England's first ally and trading partner. With Portugal's imminent entry into the Common Market, the country is about to embark upon a new era in its history and so it was an opportune moment for the State Visit as a gesture of British friendship. The first day of the visit was spent in Lisbon, the capital of Portugal, starting with the Royal party sailing up the River Tagus on the Royal Yacht *Britannia*.

(*Below and facing page*) On the first day the Queen and Prince Philip had lunch with President Eanes and his wife at Belem Palace, the President's official residence and afterwards went for a stroll in the Palace gardens. Throughout the tour the Royal party was accompanied by interpreters as the President speaks only Portuguese.

(*Left*) On the second day of the State Visit the Queen and Prince Philip travelled to Sintra, an old town renowned for its beautiful mountain location. The fifteenth-century royal palace, a favourite residence of Portuguese monarchs, was the setting for the official lunch with the Prime Minister of Portugal and Madame Soares.

(*Facing page*) Afterwards the Queen and Prince Philip visited a British-run school, St Julian's at nearby Carcavelos. Gathered on the school hockey pitch were also British schoolchildren and their parents, some 2000 in all, who had come from all over Lisbon to see the Queen.

(*Overleaf*) At the University of Evora, a former Jesuit university in this ancient Portuguese town, a traditional black cloak was placed around the Queen's shoulders by the students, a mark of great respect, as they stood on the steps of the sixteenth-century building.

(*Below*) In Evora the highlight of the visit for the Queen, who is an acknowledged expert on the breeding of horses, was the equestrian display by the Portuguese Riding School. (*Far below*) The streets of Evora were bedecked with colourful hangings and bedspreads, an ancient Portuguese tradition, for the Queen's walk through the old town.

(*Facing page*) The last day of the State Visit was spent visiting Oporto, the second largest city in Portugal. Oporto has had long links with the British as it is the home of Port wine and there is still a large British community in the city, involved with the shipping of Port. Here, the Queen and Prince Philip acknowledge the crowds as they stand on the balcony of Oporto City Hall.

In April Tim Graham was invited to take a series of photographs to mark the 21st birthday of Lady Helen Windsor, the only daughter of the Duke and Duchess of Kent. These informal photographs show Lady Helen at Lancaster House, near St James's Palace. Lady Helen now works for Christie's, the fine art auctioneers in the contemporary art department.

A Grand Tour of Italy

The English have had a love affair with Italy and the Italian way of life for many years and so it was with great enthusiasm that the Prince and Princess of Wales set off for their long visit to Italy, lasting seventeen days in all, and their first to a country outside the Commonwealth. The visit covered the length and breadth of the country, from the northern cities of Milan and Venice to the island of

Sicily in the far south and everywhere they went the Royal couple were greeted by vast crowds. The enthusiasm and determination of the Italians to greet the Prince and Princess of Wales caused the police some headaches and the cheerful, chaotic organization was much enjoyed by the Royal couple.

(*Far left and left*) The tour started at Olbia airport on the island of Sardinia where Prince Charles inspected a guard of honour. The Princess of Wales decided to be relaxed and comfortable for the important and exacting first day and wore a favourite lavender-coloured suit designed by Jan Van Velden. (*Above*) Leaving a restaurant at Porto Rotondo where the Princess of Wales had enjoyed her first taste of genuine Italian spaghetti.

(*Overleaf*) On board the Italian training ship, the *Amerigo Vespucci* at La Spezia, the chief Italian naval base at the eastern end of the Italian Riviera. The Prince and Princess of Wales had travelled overnight from Sardinia to the mainland on board the Royal Yacht *Britannia* which was used as a base for much of the trip. The Princess paid a witty compliment to the Italian navy, their hosts for the day, by wearing a tailored navy and white pinstripe coat-dress topped by a nautical-style white hat.

The highlight of the stay in Milan was a gala evening at La Scala to watch a performance of Puccini's *Turandot*. Prince Charles, a great lover of opera, was thrilled to see the inside of this world-famous opera house with its glittering red and gold auditorium.

(*Above*) Enthusiastic crowds greeting Prince Charles during a walkabout in Milan. Both the Prince and Princess of Wales had had private lessons in Italian at Kensington Palace beforehand and delighted everyone on these walkabouts with their spoken Italian. (*Right*) Sightseeing in Milan included a visit to the Cathedral of Sant'Ambrosio.

(*Left and below*) For a dinner at the Palazzo Vecchio hosted by the mayor of Florence the Princess of Wales wore a stunning black and bright blue dress decorated with shimmering silver and bright blue stars.

(*Facing page*) The Prince and Princess of Wales spent three days in Florence, the jewel of the Italian Renaissance and the country's cultural capital, including a visit to the church and monastery of San Miniato al Monte in the foothills surrounding the city.

On the second day in Florence the Princess of Wales delighted the crowds by wearing an amusing 'Italian waiter's outfit'. (*Above*) On the agenda was more sight-seeing, including a visit to the large Franciscan church of Santa Croce with its imposing main doorway.

(*Above*) On the first morning in Rome the Prince and Princess of Wales went their separate ways and, by special request, the Princess visited the main children's hospital in the city, the Hospital of Baby Jesus. She was dressed in a striking black and white outfit with a sweeping shawl collar fastened with buttons on one hip and with a black straw fez fastened with a decorative pin on her head.

(*Right*) The Prince and Princess of Wales then went together to the Casina Valadier for a lunch given by Signor Craxi, President of the European Council of Ministers.

(*Facing page*) For lunch with the President of Italy at his official residence in Rome, the Palazzo Quirinale, the Princess of Wales wore a smart, striped, tailored suit in silk seersucker designed by one of her most imaginative designers, Bruce Oldfield.

(*Above and right*) Sightseeing in Rome included visits to the Forum and to the Pantheon, two of the city's most famous sights.

From Rome the Prince and Princess of Wales travelled south to Anzio, thirty miles away, to take part in a wreath-laying ceremony at the Anzio Beach-head cemetery, the site of terrible fighting with heavy loss of life in 1944. After the ceremony the Prince of Wales, wearing the service dress uniform of the Gordon Highlanders, and the Princess of Wales walked amongst the graves of young British and American servicemen who had died during the fighting.

The private 45-minute audience with Pope John Paul II was the most significant engagement on the Royal agenda. The Prince and Princess of Wales emerged from the audience with the Pope looking relaxed and cheerful, a marked contrast to their nervousness beforehand. For the audience the Princess wore a traditional black lace dress with matching veil over her head.

Following the private audience with the Pope, the Prince and Princess of Wales spent the afternoon touring the Vatican and seeing some of its world-famous treasures, including the magnificent Sistine Chapel and St Mark's Basilica.

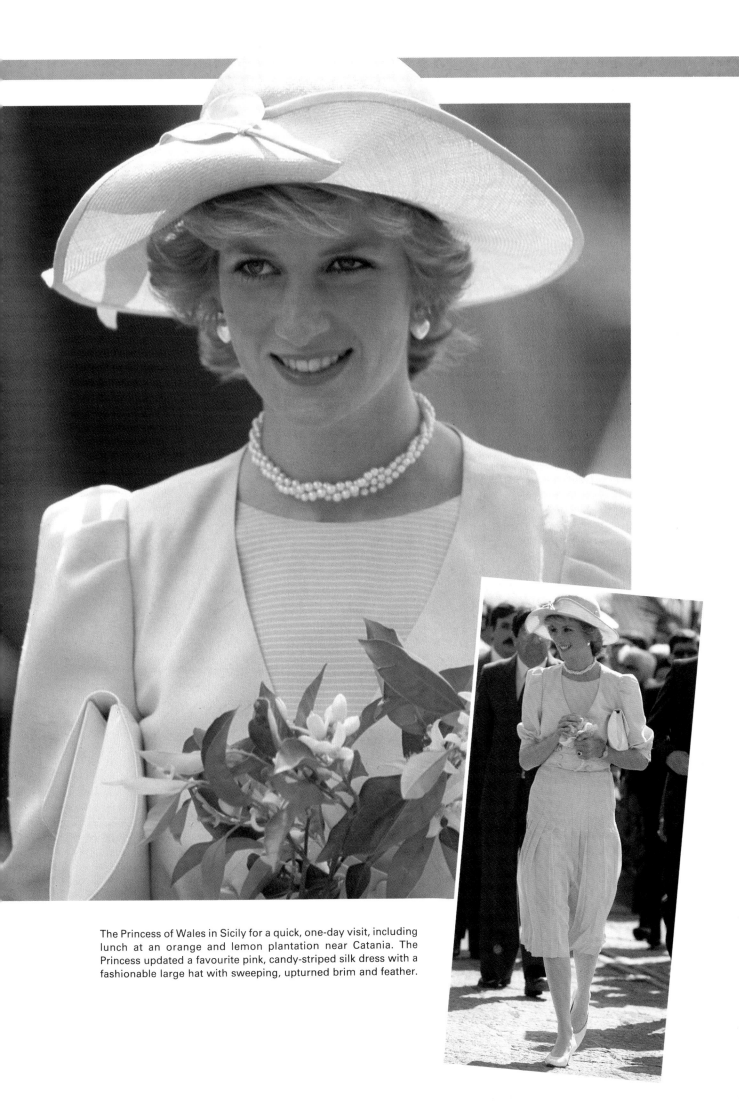

The Princess of Wales in Sicily for a quick, one-day visit, including lunch at an orange and lemon plantation near Catania. The Princess updated a favourite pink, candy-striped silk dress with a fashionable large hat with sweeping, upturned brim and feather.

The brief stop in Sicily included a tour of the famous Greek and Roman remains at Syracuse, once an important Greek city. Archaeology is one of Prince Charles's great interests and in the vast Greek amphitheatre there he showed the Princess of Wales the beauties of ancient Greek architecture.

At Syracuse the Royal party joined the Royal Yacht *Britannia* again for the sail up the Adriatic coast to Venice. On the way, the Prince and Princess of Wales visited the city of Trani and its Romanesque cathedral with its fine bronze doors.

After disembarking from the Royal Yacht, the Prince and Princess of Wales had a private tour of the Doges' Palace and went for a walkabout in St Mark's Square.

(*Overleaf*) Afterwards the Royal party set off in a launch for a trip along the Grand Canal and on to the island of Torcello for lunch at the world-famous restaurant, Cipriani's.

(*Facing page*) After church came the ceremonial ride in a Venetian gondola. Despite the light drizzle and the scores of onlookers lining the narrow banks, the Prince and Princess of Wales seemed to enjoy their four-minute ride.

(*Above*) The Princess of Wales on the way to dinner with the Mayor of Venice, the last evening engagement ashore of the long tour.

(*Right*) The Prince and Princess of Wales walking to attend Matins at St George's Anglican Church. It was a grey, damp day and the Princess kept warm in a stunning green coat-dress designed by the Emanuels.

After the long separation, the Prince and Princess of Wales enjoyed a reunion with their children who flew out to meet them in Venice at the start of a private four-day cruise on board the Royal Yacht. Prince William waved enthusiastically and Prince Henry took a cautious glance at the cheering crowds on the quayside below.

The Royal Windsor Horse Show

Windsor Great Park provides a spectacular setting for this colourful show which takes place in May. The show lasts for several days and includes dressage, carriage-driving trials and show-jumping.

Many members of the Royal Family take a keen interest in the show. This year Princess Anne and her two children, Peter and Zara Phillips came to watch Mark Phillips competing.

The Queen enjoys the company of her two eldest grandchildren, Peter Phillips, aged seven, and Zara, aged four. To her great pleasure both children, who spend most of the year living at their country home in Gloucestershire, now show a great interest in horses. At this year's Royal Windsor Horse Show they enjoyed a ride on a carriage-and-four belonging to the Queen.

The Royal Windsor Horse Show includes many driving competitions and Prince Philip is a keen participant in the team-driving trials. He is one of Britain's leading competitive drivers and was keenly watched by the Queen during the marathon course around Windsor Great Park.

Prince Michael of Kent is a newcomer to the demanding sport of carriage-driving. At this year's Royal Windsor Horse Show he drove the Queen's bay carriage horses in the class for pairs of horses.

Prince Charles, Colonel-in-Chief of the Parachute Regiment, took Prince William with him to watch the army's élite parachute team, the Red Devils make a landing in the gardens of Kensington Palace on 23 May. Prince William watched the free-fall sky-divers in amazement and afterwards had many questions to ask the Red Devils commander, Captain Mickey Munn. The landing was performed in order to launch an appeal to raise money to buy a new Islander aircraft for the team.

(*Left and below*) Princess Anne at the TI Group Windsor Horse Trials which take place each year in Windsor Great Park at the end of May. Princess Anne is President of the Three-Day Event and is also one of the hardest-working members of the organizing committee.

(*Facing page*) On 30 May the Princess of Wales paid her first official visit to the Isle of Wight. She spent a busy day in Ryde and Sandown, opening a club for the elderly and touring youth training workshops, a business centre and a fire station.

Polo is a very exciting game to watch and the Queen and the Princess of Wales often follow the matches at Smith's Lawn, Windsor, especially when the Prince of Wales is playing. Prince Charles plays mainly for two teams, high goal for Les Diables Bleus and medium goal for The Maple Leafs.

Derby Day

The Derby, which was first contested as far back as 1780, is now the most famous horse-race in the world. Derby Day is part of Britain's colourful tradition and a great day out for many Londoners as well as a grand social occasion. Both the Queen and the

Queen Mother are successful racehorse owners – the Queen's interest is in flat-racing and breeding while the Queen Mother loves steeplechasing. The Queen, a keen race-goer and one of the largest thoroughbred owners in Britain, usually takes a large party to Epsom Racecourse on Derby Day. This year the Royal party included the Queen Mother, Princess Anne and Princess Alexandra and her husband, the Hon. Angus Ogilvy.

Before the start of the Derby, the Royal party leave the Royal Box to walk to the paddock and take a closer look at some of the world's most famous racehorses. (*Left*) Princess Alexandra and the Hon. Angus Ogilvy talking to Michael Oswald, the Queen's stud manager who is in charge of breeding the Queen's thoroughbreds.

On 6 June Princess Michael of Kent, cheerful and smiling in spite of the terrible wet weather, commissioned the canal boat *Challenge* on behalf of the Docklands Canal Boat Trust at Bow in East London.

(*Below*) The Queen and the President of Mexico leaving Victoria Station for the traditional State Drive back to Buckingham Palace at the start of the President's State Visit to Britain in June. (*Right*) Princess Alexandra and the Hon. Angus Ogilvy were part of the Royal party who welcomed the President at the start of the State Visit.

(*Below*) The Prince of Wales in No 1 dress uniform of the 5th Royal Inniskilling Dragoon Guards. In the spring of 1985 Prince Charles was appointed the regiment's new Colonel-in-Chief and on 12 June he paid his first visit to the regiment, currently stationed at Tidworth in Wiltshire, for the Presentation of a new Standard as well as to celebrate the regiment's tercentenary this year. (*Left*) The official ceremony over, Prince Charles changed into simple barrack dress in order to have a go at driving a Chieftain tank.

The Prince and Princess of Wales at the European première of the 14th James Bond film, *A View to a Kill*, at the Odeon, Leicester Square. The première was in aid of the Prince's Trust and the British Deaf Association whose patron is the Princess of Wales. (*Below left*) Accompanying the Royal couple for the evening were Prince Albert of Monaco and Roger Moore's daughter, Deborah.

(*Above*) Princess Anne attending a fête at Jesus College, Cambridge on 13 June. The fête was organized by volunteers of the Cambridgeshire and South Lincolnshire branches of Save the Children Fund whose President is Princess Anne. As well as her much-publicized overseas tours on behalf of the Fund, the Princess, an extremely hard-working President, visits many of the Fund's projects and fund-raising events at home in Britain.

(*Right*) For the return journey to London by helicopter Princess Anne met up with Prince Philip who had also been in Cambridge in his capacity as Chancellor of Cambridge University.

The Falklands Memorial Service

In June the Queen and other members of the Royal Family attended a service at St Paul's Cathedral to dedicate a memorial to those who had died during the Falklands Conflict three years earlier.

(*Right*) Princess Anne and Prince Andrew leaving St Paul's Cathedral after the Service. (*Below*) The Queen being escorted from St Paul's by Sir Alan Traill, the Lord Mayor of London. (*Facing page*) The Prince and Princess of Wales leaving St Paul's.

Members of the Royal Family leaving St Paul's Cathedral after the Falklands Memorial Service. (*Facing page*) The Duke and Duchess of Kent. The Duke is wearing the No 1 dress uniform of Colonel of the Scots Guards. (*Right*) Princess Alice Duchess of Gloucester with her daughter-in-law the Duchess of Gloucester. (*Below*) Prince Michael of Kent, wearing the No 1 dress uniform of a major in The Royal Hussars, with his sister Princess Alexandra.

(*Overleaf*) The Queen riding sidesaddle on her way to Horse Guards Parade for the ceremony of Trooping the Colour. The ceremonious trooping of the colour to mark the reigning monarch's official birthday began in 1755 under George II and has continued ever since. During the present Queen's reign it has been held on the second Saturday in June. In 1985 it was the turn of the 2nd Battalion Coldstream Guards to troop their colour and the Queen is therefore wearing the uniform of Colonel-in-Chief of the Coldstream Guards.

After Trooping the Colour is over the Queen's official birthday is then marked by a flypast of The Royal Air Force down the Mall and over the roof of Buckingham Palace. To watch the spectacular flypast the Queen leads the Royal Family, including many of the younger generation, out onto the Palace balcony. This year saw the first appearance of Prince Henry, carried in turn by his parents.

The Garter Day Ceremony

Royal Ascot Week in the middle of June. The Most Noble Order of the Garter, dedicated to St George, the patron saint of England, was founded by Edward III in 1348 and the Order's procession from Windsor Castle to St George's Chapel for the annual Service is a magnificent scene of pageantry which many people come to watch.

This is one of the oldest traditions of Britain and takes place at Windsor Castle at the beginning of

(*Below*) After the Service is over, the Queen and other members of the Royal Family return to Windsor Castle by carriage. The Queen, as Sovereign, is Head of the Order and the appointment of the twenty-four Knights of the Garter is her choice alone. (*Facing page*) With the addition of black velvet hats with ostrich plumes, the distinctive dress has remained unchanged since the reign of Charles II in the seventeenth century. The first Tudor king, Henry VII added the Collar or gold chain, consisting of Tudor roses to which is attached the pendant badge called 'the George'.

(*Right*) The Prince and Princess of Wales returning to Windsor Castle after the Garter Day Service at St George's Chapel. By tradition the Prince of Wales is a Knight of the Garter and Prince Charles was installed in 1978. (*Above*) The Queen Mother accompanied by the King of Sweden. As a former Queen Consort the Queen Mother is a Lady of the Garter. Foreign royalty have long been appointed members of the Order with the title of 'Stranger Knight'. The Queen appointed the King of Sweden a member of the Order on her State visit to Sweden in 1984 and this was the King's first appearance at the ceremony.

The Royal Meeting in June at Ascot is the highlight of the summer season, both as a sporting occasion and as a social one, with the elegant fashions, especially on Ladies' Day, attracting almost as much attention as the famous thoroughbred horses. The Royal Family traditionally attend the four-day meeting. (*Above*) The Princess of Wales escorted by Prince Andrew, home on leave from the Royal Navy. (*Left*) The Princess of Wales accompanied by her bodyguard as she makes her way through the vast crowds.

(*Right*) The Duchess of Gloucester. At the Royal Meeting before the start of each afternoon's racing, the Royal party drive up the course in landaus. The Queen heads the procession, followed by other members of the Royal Family and guests staying at Windsor Castle for the week. (*Below*) The Queen Mother is a favourite of the crowds at Royal Ascot.

(*Facing page*) The Queen at Royal Ascot surrounded by a sea of hats.

During the Royal Meeting hats are obligatory for ladies in the Royal Enclosure and the beautifully dressed Royal ladies set the tone for this elegant social event. (*Left*) The Duchess of Kent. (*Facing page*) Princess Margaret.

Prince Andrew in Canada

Canada and the Canadians now enjoy a special relationship with Prince Andrew who has visited the country on many occasions. His first visit was in 1976 to watch his sister, Princess Anne compete in the XXI Olympic Games in Montreal. The following year he returned to spend two terms at Lakefield College, Ontario, one of Canada's outstanding boys' boarding schools. The nine-day tour at the end of June was a goodwill visit and covered three provinces, New Brunswick, Nova Scotia and Ontario. The visit began at Fredericton, the capital of New Brunswick, called Canada's 'Picture Province'.

(*Left*) Prince Andrew inspecting the Guard of Honour outside the Legislative Assembly Building in Fredericton. He is accompanied by the Guard Commander and behind, by his Canadian Equerry. (*Below*) Prince Andrew replying to the address of welcome to New Brunswick by the Premier before entering the Legislative Assembly Building, the seat of government for New Brunswick.

(*Left*) Prince Andrew at Fredericton on board the motor yacht *Via Mara* for a cruise on the Saint John River, the largest river in the province.

(*Facing page above*) On his walkabout in Fredericton Prince Andrew was presented with almost as many flowers as the Princess of Wales receives on her walkabouts. (*Facing page below*) Prince Andrew face to face with 'a green animal' at the Canada Games Stadium in Saint John, New Brunswick.

(*Right*) Prince Andrew is a qualified helicopter pilot and helped pilot the Canadian Forces helicopter which took him from Saint John to Sussex, New Brunswick for a civic welcome and a barbecue.

(*Facing page*) Prince Andrew taking his turn at the wheel of *Bluenose II* in Halifax Harbour, Nova Scotia.

(*Left*) At the barbecue in Sussex given by the Premier of New Brunswick in the 8th Hussars Sports Centre Prince Andrew took part in a horseshoe-throwing demonstration. (*Below*) Before the barbecue Prince Andrew toured a small livestock show and cheerfully greeted this prize-winning Jersey cow.

(*Facing page*) Prince Andrew in Nova Scotia. During the tour Prince Andrew delighted the Canadians by his relaxed but impeccable behaviour.

In the Western Isles

As well as being the Prince of Wales, Prince Charles is also Lord of the Isles, a title which refers to the wild and rugged collection of islands in the north-west of Scotland called the Western Isles or, more familiarly, the Outer Hebrides. In July the Prince and Princess of Wales spent three days touring the islands. Despite the very wet and windy weather the Royal couple enjoyed every minute of their visit.

(*Left*) Striding out on Great Bernera. Being carried behind Prince Charles is the salmon he had just caught from a salmon cage. (*Facing page*) The Princess of Wales holding flowers presented to her on the island of Great Bernera. The Princess came prepared for the grey weather and on the first day of the visit wore a check, velvet-trimmed suit rather than summer silks.

(*Below*) Coping with the weather, the Royal party on their way to lunch at Kiessimul Castle on the island of Barra.

(*Left*) Walking on North Uist, amid much cheering by the islanders who had turned out in force. (*Below*) North Uist boasts a high percentage of twins and at a gathering at Lochmaddy the Prince and Princess of Wales were introduced to thirty-six pairs of them.

(*Facing page*) Applauding a display of Hebridean dancing at Castlebay, Barra.

(*Facing page*) The Princess of Wales at Ardveenish on the Island of Barra, well wrapped up against the Hebridean weather.

(*Right*) The Prince and Princess of Wales arrive by helicopter at Bayhead, North Uist for the start of the third and final day of their Scottish tour.

(*Below*) The Royal party setting out to inspect shellfish and salmon cages at Lochmaddy, North Uist.

(*Overleaf*) The Princess of Wales presenting the Prince of Wales with first prize at a charity polo match in July in aid of Birthright, one of the Princess's favourite charities.

This edition first published in Great Britain in 1985
for Marks and Spencer by Park Lane Press,
40 Park Street, London W1Y 4DE

Designer: Colin Reed
Text set by SX Composing Ltd, Rayleigh, Essex
Colour originated by Bridge Graphics Ltd, Hull
Printed and bound by Severn Valley Press Ltd, Caerphilly, Wales